IMAGES
of America

LOS ANGELES
CALIFORNIA

IMAGES
of America

LOS ANGELES
CALIFORNIA

Portia Lee and Jeffrey Samudio

ARCADIA
PUBLISHING

Published by Arcadia Publishing
Charleston, South Carolina

Library of Congress Catalog Card Number: 2001086325

For all general information contact Arcadia Publishing at:
Telephone 843-853-2070
Fax 843-853-0044
E-mail sales@arcadiapublishing.com
For customer service and orders:
Toll-Free 1-888-313-2665

Visit us on the Internet at www.arcadiapublishing.com

CONTENTS

ACKNOWLEDGMENTS

The images in this volume have been drawn from the Architectural Slide Collection of the University of Southern California. Our thanks are due them in great measure. Images from private collections and other organizations are acknowledged below. We have attempted to include as many of postcard images as possible. These original images, taken between 1910 and 1915, document views of Los Angeles that were intended to show the city in its very best light and actively recruit new residents and tourists to the city, but not every postcard was commercial in nature. Many of these small images were simply mementos. Today they offer valuable insights into the culture and character of Los Angeles captured in a moment of past time.

Chapter 1
p. 14 (1) Badger Avenue Bridge: Collection of the Port of Los Angeles
p. 14 (2) Badger Avenue Bridge Tender's Cabin: Collection of California Archives, Los Angeles

Chapter 2
p. 15 Terra Cotta Frieze, Washington Boulevard Bridge: Archives of the City of Los Angeles
p. 16 Old Seventh Street Bridge, Collection of the Bureau of Engineering, City of Los Angeles
p. 17 Seventh Street Viaduct: Regional History Collection/University of Southern California
p. 18 Glendale Hyperion Viaduct: Security Pacific Collection/Los Angeles Public Library
p. 19-20 Macy Street Bridge: Security Pacific Collection: Los Angeles Public Library
p. 21 North Broadway Bridge: Regional History Collection/University of Southern California
p. 22 First Street Bridge: Regional History Collection/University of Southern California

Chapter 14
p. 117 The Montenegro Family, Shades of L.A. Collection/Los Angeles Public Library
p. 118 (1) Los Angeles City Engineer's Survey Team: Archives of the City of Los Angeles
p. 118 (2) Collection of the African-American Firefighter's Museum, Los Angeles
p. 119 Nellie Kay Carlisle: Collection of Alma Carlisle, Los Angeles
p. 120 Shinto Temple, Terminal Island, Security Pacific Collection/Los Angeles Public Library
p. 121 Cannery Workers, Terminal Island: Security Pacific Collection/Los Angeles Public Library
p. 122 Betty and Betsy; Collection of Betty R. Quon, Glendale, California
p. 123 (1) The Gomez Family, Shades of L.A. Collection/Los Angeles Public Library
p. 123 (2) Lil;lie Gomez, Shades of L.A. Collection/Los Angeles Public Library
p. 124 Richard Keyes Biggs: Collection of Jelil Romano, Los Angeles
p. 125 (1) Harriette Carr Von Breton: Collection of June Holroyd, Santa Barbara, California
p. 127 (1) Air Passenger: Collection of Glen Dean Jones, Riverside
p. 127 (2) Air Passenger: Collection of Glen Dean Jones, Riverside

The following publications provided invaluable historic and bibliographic resources:

Banham, Reyner, *Los Angeles: The Architecture of Four Ecologies.* The Penguin Press, 1976
Comer, Virginia L., Los Angeles: *A View From Crown Hill.* Talbot Press, 1986
Gebhard, David and Robert Winter, *Los Angeles: An Architectural Guide.* Gibbs Smith, Salt Lake City, 1994
Gebhard, David and Harriette Von Breton, *Los Angeles in the Thirties.* Hennessey & Ingalls, Inc., Los Angeles 1989
Gleye, Paul, *The Architecture of Los Angeles.* Rosebud Books, Los Angeles, 1981
Kahrl, William L., *Water and Power.* University of California Press, Berkeley, 1982
Kaplan, Sam Hall, *LA Lost and Found.* Crown Paperbacks, 1987
Pitt, Leonard and Dale Pitt, *Los Angeles A to Z.* University of California Press, Berkeley, 1997.
Queenan, Charles F., *The Port of Los Angeles: From Wilderness to World Port.* Los Angeles Harbor Department, 1983
Robinson, W.W., *Land in California.* University of California Press, Berkeley, 1948

We are also indebted to Hynda Rudd and Jay Jones of the Los Angeles City Archives and Carolyn Kozo Cole of the Los Angeles Public Library Photo Collection. Mark Wanamaker of Bison Archives provided great help with Hollywood historical references, John Heller shared his knowledge on street railways and Alma Carlisle gave timely assistance with the African American historical photos. We shall always remember with immense gratitude the contribution of the late Thomas Owen to the California Index of the Los Angeles Central Library, and his lifelong dedication to documenting the theater history and culture of the city of Los Angeles.

INTRODUCTION

Images of Los Angeles records a community that established itself as it grew exponentially. Neither natural disasters nor financial losses daunted the first settlers or discouraged the new arrivals who sought the chance to begin again in a new city. Los Angeles city-makers had in mind an ideal city and in its construction they demonstrated innovation and energy. In 1900 Los Angeles had been an American city for fifty years; in another fifty it would be a metropolis.

Los Angeles was founded in 1781 as one of the two original Spanish pueblos in California, making it entitled by law to four square leagues of land. Set in a valley of the Los Angeles River, the pueblo was intended as a supply base for the garrisons stationed in Southern California. While it had been granted city status by the Mexican government in 1835, sixty years after its founding, the pueblo of Los Angeles was still a small cattle market town surrounded by ranchos with immense acreage. The city began to reconsider its "cow town" condition in 1851 when statehood and the United States Board of Land Commissioners required it to prove its claims to city lands.

At the hearing before the Land Commission, Los Angeles made a startling argument. It claimed not just four square leagues, but sixteen, as historian W.W. Robinson says, "longing even then to be the biggest city." The Mayor and Council attorneys argued that the law governing the establishment of the pueblo as four square leagues actually meant four leagues square, 112 square miles. The city's argument did not prevail. Los Angeles' claim was denied and the city had to be content with the original grant.

The longing to be the biggest city did not go unrealized for long. Transcontinental rail service was established by 1881. New settlers required new land; new land required water. Los Angeles had prior rights to the waters that passed through the pueblo boundaries and it was willing to share it - with those inside the boundaries. The price of water for neighboring cities was annexation. First in were 904 acres on the former northeastern pueblo boundary; then the Shoestring Annexation of 1909 that brought Los Angeles its harbor. The Hollywood consolidation of 1910 brought population and the fledgling movie industry to a town that needed a sewer as well as water for households. By 1945 the small town that had begun with 28 square miles had grown to 450 square miles through 95 annexations. Robinson sums it up well: "Fifty foot lots, stuccoed houses, filling stations, shops, food markets, and heavy traffic filled the Los Angeles panorama."

The images in this book document the buildings and community members of those eventful fifty years. Sometimes disappointed, or unfairly cheated by circumstances, but always-hard working and resourceful, the citizens of Los Angeles built their communities. Businessmen constructed a downtown streetscape whose architecture excited envy in other cities. Hotels catered to visitors with such boosterism that the travelers would go home, pack up and return with sufficient capital for an ambitious scheme of their own. The introduction of the car into the mix allowed for mobility and a brand new outlook on life. Los Angeles became a drive-in city, laid out the freeway system and decided not to ride on streetcars any more. Angelenos had fun shopping, at the movies, in the eateries, and motoring on Wilshire Boulevard.

In a temperamental moment, Frank Lloyd Wright opined, "It's as if you tipped the United States up so that all the commonplace people slid down into Southern California." Perhaps they did slide down, and hit the ground running too, intent on doing uncommon things in rather spectacular ways and looking sensational while it happened. From aqueducts to skyscrapers, the builders constructed the city that promised a place in the sun for everyone. The images of this book record journeys of a half-century—a short, bumpy, adventurous ride.

ST. VIBIANA'S ORGAN. This four manual Wangerin was the original organ of St. Vibiana's Cathedral. Built in 1876, the church was the seat of the Los Angeles Archdiocese. This organ was replaced in a 1922 remodeling of the church. After its marble interior furnishings, Judson Studio stained glass windows, pews, and organ were removed, St. Vibiana's was closed in 1997.

One

BUILDING AN AQUEDUCT
CREATING A HARBOR

In 1899, the City of Los Angeles, citing the Spanish grant to the pueblo in 1781, won a court decision affirming its exclusive rights to all water sources in the Los Angeles Basin. Before European exploration, the 58-mile Los Angeles River supported an extensive wetland. The valleys between the San Gabriel and Santa Monica Mountains formed its watershed, sending streams flowing southward into the Basin. Converging near present day Elysian Park, a high water table created marshlands, ponds, and a lush vegetation cover.

Alternate cycles of flood and drought meant an undependable supply of an indispensable resource, persuading the city makers of the turn of the century that only a reliable water supply would guarantee the city's growth to a critical mass necessary for prosperity. As the 20th century dawned in Los Angeles, growth was the game and no one could play without a stake of water. "Whoever brings the water will bring the people," stated Chief Engineer and Superintendent William Mulholland of the Los Angeles City Water Company. Los Angeles reached into the eastern Sierra Nevada Mountains to capture the water of the Owens River, setting a pattern of ruthless resource appropriation for development in the city.

SAN FRANCISQUITO POWER PLANT NO. 1 OF THE OWENS RIVER AQUEDUCT. William Mulholland supervised 5,000 workers in the 6-year construction of the 233-mile Los Angeles Aqueduct. A bond election in 1910 provided the first public funds for the construction of ancillary municipal hydroelectric plants.

9

CONSTRUCTION WORKERS INSIDE PIPELINE, OWENS RIVER AQUEDUCT. All workers on the pipelines were under Mulholland's supervision; no private contractors undertook the work. Although consulting engineers feared a labor shortage, 4,000 tunnellers and diggers set to work in 1907 as city employees.

Owens River Aqueduct, Water Supply Pipes. A system of bonuses compensated workers who exceeded the daily quota set up by Mulholland. Crews worked 12 hours and sometimes through shifts when water flooded tunnels. Temperatures were cooler below the surface, but cave-ins, rockslides, and water flooding into tunnels made the operation perilous.

Owens River Aqueduct, Filling the Baldwin Hills Reservoir. Water from the Owens River Project spurred development in the city's outlying territories. Water from San Francisquito Dam filled a reservoir dug in the Baldwin Hills, lands south of downtown near present day Culver City.

OWENS RIVER AQUEDUCT, SERPENTINE PIPELINE. Pipes, siphons, tunnels, dams, and reservoirs advanced toward the city as relentlessly as the population burgeoned. "In the story of the Aqueduct," writes historian William L. Kahrl, "we confront the foundations of the modern metropolis of California."

SAN PEDRO HARBOR. Los Angeles, situated on neither a navigable river nor the sea, created a harbor by dredging the mud flats and salt marshes of San Pedro Bay, 25 miles south of downtown. After 1910 when Wilmington and San Pedro were annexed to Los Angeles, the Federal Government and Los Angeles deepened channels, built breakwaters, and maintained a lighthouse at Pt. Fermin. This photo, c. 1900, shows harbor construction using rock quarried from nearby Catalina Island.

SAN PEDRO HARBOR WITH SUBMARINES. In 1908 the Great White Fleet of the United States Navy anchored inside the partially completed breakwater of the port, bringing with them a small group of submarines. By 1912 the first section of the San Pedro Harbor breakwater was completed, the main channel widened and dredged to 30 feet.

THE BADGER AVENUE (HENRY FORD) BRIDGE. Designed by famed engineer Joseph B. Strauss, the bridge connected Wilmington to the north side of Terminal Island in Los Angeles harbor. Straus modernized the construction of the bascule, a variant of the medieval drawbridge. When opened in 1924, the structure stretched 760-feet across the Cerritos Channel with walkways for pedestrian traffic, rail lines for Santa Fe and Union Pacific freight traffic, and a street railway track. The structure was taken down in 1997 and replaced with a suspension bridge.

BRIDGE TENDER'S CONTROL CABIN, THE BADGER AVENUE (HENRY FORD) BRIDGE. The bridge tender sat in this small cabin at the end of the bridge manipulating the levers that raised and lowered the twin leaves of the bascule when ocean going traffic passed. When train traffic passed over the bridge, the tender was required to go onto the bridge to lock the rail sections in place. In this view taken from the control cabin, the rail roadway, visible through the cabin window, rises to the perpendicular as the bascule lifts.

14

Two

BRIDGES OVER
THE WATERS

With the construction of the North Broadway Bridge in 1911, downtown Los Angeles was linked with the commercial and residential communities east of the waterway. By the 1920s the city's extensive street railway system extended outward in a 30-mile radius and the decorative light pedestals of the bridges were designed with tall poles to carry trolley wires.

A two million dollar bond issue in 1924 enabled Chief Engineer of Bridges Merrill Butler to construct a set of highly ornamented crossings in arch rib reinforced concrete. The Los Angeles Municipal Arts Commission approved the river bridges design, guided by the philosophy of the City Beautiful Movement: the monumental crossings would promote pride in government and demonstrate the City's commitment to progress.

A dry bed in summer, the Los Angeles River became a torrent in rich water years. Debris flows from its headwaters in the San Gabriel Mountains swept down the channel, toppling trestle bridges and swamping railway causeways. The public demanded high, all-weather crossings. The floods of 1934 and 1938 doomed the river and flood control construction set the river's banks in concrete. Today only 17 percent of its streambed has sandy bottom and native vegetation.

TERRA COTTA FRIEZE, WASHINGTON BOULEVARD BRIDGE. Opened in 1931, Washington Boulevard featured an ornamental light pedestal at each corner of the viaduct. The orange and black tiles of the Art Deco frieze depicted men and machines at work in the building of the bridge.

15

OLD SEVENTH STREET TRESTLE BRIDGE. Old Seventh Street, an unsightly and flood-prone crossing, was swept away in the flood of 1905. It connected the main residential suburb of Boyle Heights, situated east of the river, with the downtown core of Los Angeles.

SEVENTH STREET VIADUCT, 1910 AND 1927. Old Seventh Street Bridge was replaced with an arch rib reinforced concrete, earth-filled structure in 1910. In 1927 a superstructure was built on top of the original arches, which were retained and used as a base for columns that supported the girder spans of the new longer viaduct. Baluster handrails, incised piers, and combination trolley wire poles and lampposts ornamented the structure.

VICTORY MEMORIAL BRIDGE—GLENDALE-HYPERION VIADUCT. Dedicated in 1919 as the Victory Memorial Bridge, Glendale-Hyperion Viaduct honored Los Angeles members of the American Expeditionary Forces in Europe during World War I. Austere conical towers and cast bronze light standards with globes shaped as candles echo the memorial theme of the bridge.

179   GLENDALE-HYPERION VIADUCT, LOS ANGELES, CALIFORNIA

GLENDALE HYPERION VIADUCT. A complex of three crossings and a street railway bridge, Glendale Hyperion solved a difficult problem of traffic congestion on the main artery from Los Angeles to the neighboring city of Glendale. Its wooded west approach on the Los Angeles side of the river was located in Griffith Park. The Pacific Electric bridge is shown at right.

18

THE MACY STREET BRIDGE (CESAR CHAVEZ AVENUE) AT WINTER FLOOD TIDE. Named in honor of Dr. Obed Macy, one of the city's pioneering physicians, the Macy Street Bridge was located at the intersection of the river and the traditional road of the Franciscan Mission fathers, El Camino Real. In 1997, the bridge's connector road was renamed Cesar Chavez Avenue in honor of the founder of the Farm Workers Union.

MACY STREET BRIDGE (CESAR CHAVEZ AVENUE) AFTER THE STORM. The choice of Spanish Colonial Revival architectural elements was intended to memorialize the city's Hispanic heritage and acknowledge the small band of priest and settlers, *padres* and *pobladores*, who founded the city in 1789. The Los Angeles City seal is displayed at the corner of the massive piers

THE NORTH BROADWAY BRIDGE (BUENA VISTA VIADUCT). Intended to be seen from passenger railroad cars on the riverbed below and from Elysian Park on the north, the structure had elaborated consoles and engaged pillars on the arch rib spandrels. The structure, which lost much of its ornament in the 1930s, was seismically retrofitted and historically restored in 1997.

THE NORTH BROADWAY BRIDGE (BUENA VISTA VIADUCT). The first of the grand style river bridges, the Buena Vista Viaduct, later renamed the North Broadway Bridge, was designed by leading Los Angeles architect Alfred F. Rosenheim in 1911. It featured hexagonal handrail balusters, pedestrian viewing bays, and 37-foot tall paired Ionic entrance columns topped by a fanciful Doric entablature.

THE FIRST STREET BRIDGE. First Street Bridge was designed in Classical Revival style and featured massive pylons in the form of the Roman triumphal arch. Bronze tablets placed on the central pylons on each side of the roadway show the profile of bridge engineer and designer Henry G. Parker. The tablets read: *FIRST ST. VIADUCT Dedicated to the memory of HENRY G. PARKER Bridge Engineer of the City of Los Angeles 1904–1909. He lost his life in the performance of his duty.* The Los Angeles City Hall, then the tallest building in the city, towers in the right background.

Three

HOTELS

"Much of downtown Los Angeles by the 1890s," writes architectural historian Paul Gleye, "was a Queen Anne streetscape of bay windows and dramatic turrets, especially at street corners." The city did not stay with this imported national style long. Architects and builders put their own individual stamp on the city's built environment. Early hotels like the Alexandria and the Lankersheim were built by men whose interests were in real estate development and business enterprises. Since these activities were dependent on an ever-growing population base, it became important to impress the visitor with the opportunities in Los Angeles. As the city expanded, builders catered to new ideas in lifestyles for both visitors and permanent residents, giving rise to elegant downtown residential hotels and the garden hotel for the guest who wanted something that took advantage of the Los Angeles climate.

THE HOLLENBECK HOTEL. The Hollenbeck was a prominent tourist hotel around the turn of the century. It advertised to eastern travelers through its climatic orientation, stating that most rooms faced east and south so that the early morning sun would warm rooms to a pleasant summer temperature even in winter. The Hollenbeck's bay windows and turrets were a city landmark until the structure was demolished in 1932.

THE ALEXANDRIA HOTEL. The Alexandria, the city's first fireproof class-A hotel, opened in 1906. It soon became a premier tourist destination. This postcard with its American flags, banners flying and massed band, indicates an important occasion, perhaps a presidential visit. This is certainly probable since the Alexandria provided hospitality for Theodore Roosevelt, William Howard Taft, and Woodrow Wilson.

Marble Lobby, Alexandria Hotel. This c. 1910 postcard depicts the elaborate marble lobby of the Hotel Alexandria. Unable to meet the competition as hotels moved west to more fashionable districts, the Alexandria's fame receded and it was closed. Redecorated and modernized, it reopened in 1938. The marble lobby is still substantially intact.

THE ANGELUS HOTEL, c. 1905. The Angelus Hotel had the characteristic style of an upscale downtown traveler's hotel. Wrought iron balconies must have been welcomed by its visitors as a dramatic change from conventional stuffy rooms. An elaborate entrance provided another ornamental accent.

HOTEL LANKERSHIM, C. 1905. The Hotel Lankershim, at the corner of 7th and Broadway, was built by J.B. Lankershim, whose family had far-ranging agricultural interests. They invested their profits in downtown real estate and later developed portions of the San Fernando Valley. The Lankershim stood on the southeast corner of 7th and Broadway, catercorner from Bullocks department store.

BALTIMORE HOTEL. The Baltimore Hotel at Fifth and Main was positioned to attract visitors to the downtown area and nearby financial district.

THE COMMODORE HOTEL. The Commodore Hotel, located in a residential area west of downtown, operated as a residence hotel.

THE BILTMORE HOTEL FACING PERSHING SQUARE. This view from Pershing Square Park looks northwest toward the Biltmore. Constructed in 1928, the Biltmore Hotel soon became and remains today the most important historic downtown hotel. The E-shaped, 13-story structure has eclectic revival architectural details with white terra cotta at the top and ground story and red-brick facing. Balconies are a feature of the upper floors. Off the lobby is the Fifth Street Corridor, which has traditionally functioned as an interior shopping street or galleria. The ceiling of many of the ground floor meeting rooms were painted by Los Angeles artist-decorator Anthony Heinsbergen.

THE ABBEY HOTEL. The Abbey at Sixth and Figueroa Street described its location on the postcard with the legend, on "Highway 99". Located at Eighth and Figueroa, the building attracted visitors' attention with its elaborate Art Deco ornamentation.

THE TOWN HOUSE. The Town House on Wilshire Boulevard opposite LaFayette Park was a grand, full-service residential hotel with a pool and tennis courts. Built at Los Angeles' original height limit of 13 stories, the hotel had an underground garage for its tenant's cars, an innovation in 1928 that reflected the development of Wilshire Boulevard as a district of elite businesses, churches, and residences dependent on the automobile. The structure is listed on the California Register of Historic Places.

AMBASSADOR HOTEL GROUNDS. The vine-covered pergola entrance to the hotel emphasized the hotel's garden ambiance. The structure located on what was to become the most prominent and elegant neighborhood west of downtown was Los Angeles' unique version of a country hotel in an urban environment.

HE AMBASSADOR HOTEL. The Ambassador Hotel, built 1919–1921, is an expansive structure surrounded by cottages and sited far back from the street behind a vast expanse of lawn. Like the Biltmore, it hosted early Academy Award banquets. The Coconut Grove ballroom was famous throughout the United States for its Saturday night broadcasts of the popular jazz and swing era bands performing at the hotel. The structure remains, but is closed.

Four

TRANSPORTATION
GETTING THERE FROM HERE

Los Angeles' city-builders never doubted that transportation was the key to success. Historian Virginia Cromer related an impression of a new resident in the neighborhood of Crown Hill west of downtown in the first decade of the 20th century: "There were not many cars at the time on the Hill; travel was by foot. Los Angeles Railway's yellow carline or the big red cars for longer distances." When the development of Silver Lake Reservoir made development on the Hill feasible, landowner Joseph Witmer hired San Francisco cable builder Andrew Hallidie to build a car line running from Second and Spring Street downtown to insure successful subdivision of his 600-acre parcel. Transportation was for fun as well, and Angelenos never tired of jaunts to the country to explore their beautiful new home. However, the lure of the auto was becoming increasingly hard to resist, and it demanded increasing investment in infrastructure for tunnels and roadways. An excellent shuttle, the motor car, and its cousin the truck, also offered reliable access to water and rail transportation.

INCLINE STATION, LOS ANGELES AND MT. WASHINGTON RAILWAY. Los Angeles and Mount Washington Railway built an attractive Mission Revival building at the Incline Station complete with refreshment bar for waiting passengers. The line continued upward to the Mount Washington Hotel where visitors could stroll through the expansive gardens and enjoy a panoramic view of Los Angeles.

31

COURT FLIGHT 1905. Another less well-known Los Angeles funicular was Court Flight. Located on Broadway between First and Temple Streets, it raised passengers up the steep slope from Broadway to Court Street, just below the summit on Hill Street. Built in 1904, the facility burned in 1943.

TROLLEY LINE AND POPPIES, 1904. This 1904 postcard celebrates the aromatic, bright orange state flower. These pleasure-seekers on the way to Mt. Lowe rumbled out to the bright fields in the pristine countryside of the San Gabriel foothills.

HILL STREET TUNNEL, BUNKER HILL. Downtown Los Angeles' topography was as opportunistic as the aims of its citizens. Sloping upward from the west bank of the Los Angeles River, the terrain presented a set of arroyos and rolling hills moving west from downtown. One of the most formidable geographic barriers was Bunker Hill. Continued progress westward was necessary and by 1909 a tunnel had been bored through the Hill.

ANGEL'S FLIGHT. For easy access up Bunker Hill to the fashionable mansions on its sides, Angel's Flight Railway was constructed. A short funicular, it traveled 335 feet with a 33% grade. The charge for a ride in 1910 was a penny. Bunker Hill was effectively leveled for redevelopment in 1970; Angel's Flight was moved a block away and then restored for service in 1995.

33

MOUNT LOWE RAILWAY CIRCULAR BRIDGE. Balloonist S.C. Lowe, whose profession precluded any fear of flight or heights, determined to share the thrill of aerial suspension with Angelenos. Hiring cable car builder Andrew Hallidie, Lowe put into operation in 1893 The Great Incline to scale the foothills of the San Gabriel Mountains. The inaugural ascent on the Fourth of July brought passengers 1,500 feet from a pavilion in Rubio Canyon 2,000 feet above sea level with a 60% grade to the summit of Echo Mountain. 127 curves and 18 trestles later, the invigorated passengers arrived at the 5,000-foot summit which offered a restaurant, hotel and cabins. The Circular Bridge, a tight curve of railway track, offered unparalleled views of Pasadena and Altadena, if the rider wasn't afraid to look. The rail line ran until 1938 although the facilities were destroyed earlier in fires and floods on the mountain.

OPENING OF LOS ANGELES SUBWAY IN 1926. In 1926 the Pacific Electric Railway had an ambitious plan for a Los Angeles subway to provide rapid access to downtown from the west side and San Fernando Valley. A tunnel begun in 1924 ran from First Street and Glendale Boulevard to an underground station at Fourth and Hill Streets below the Subway Terminal Building.

SUBWAY TERMINAL BUILDING. The elegance and architectural distinction of the Beaux Arts Subway Terminal Building, designed by Los Angeles architects Schultz and Weaver in 1926, declared the importance of transportation to Los Angeles . The building was essentially a prestigious downtown office building whose lobby served as a street railway concourse.

BUILDING THE SUBWAY TERMINAL BUILDING. This 1919 photo shows facilities operating on Hill Street during the planning of the Subway Terminal Building.

WAITING ROOM, PACIFIC ELECTRIC RAILWAY BUILDING. The Pacific Electric Railway Building at Sixth and Main Street had a service concourse open 24 hours a day. Its impressive waiting room with classical pillars and arched door opening received outdoor light from a wire glass ceiling. All cars left from this station except those going westward to beach cities and north to Glendale and Burbank, which originated at the Subway Terminal Building.

LA GRANDE STATION, SANTA FE RAILWAY. The Moorish Revival style La Grande Station of the Santa Fe Railway opened with great fanfare on July 29, 1893. More than 50 trains daily departed from the station, which stood on Santa Fe Avenue between First and Second Streets. The main depot, 350 feet in length, had a central domed rotunda, tile floors, and a stained glass window. An adjoining garden had a landscaped, kite-shaped walk and a miniature replica of the Santa Fe's excursion route to San Bernadino, planted in palms.

SOUTHERN PACIFIC DEPOT. In April 1881, Los Angeles' centennial year, Southern Pacific Railroad, having driven south to Los Angeles, turned east to reach El Paso, Texas. In the following December it connected with the westbound Texas Pacific. At last Los Angeles was the western terminus of a transcontinental railroad. This stately Beaux Arts station replaced the first Southern Pacific "Arcade" Station.

UNION STATION PASSENGER TERMINAL, ALAMEDA AND SUNSET BOULEVARDS, LOOKING WEST TOWARD CITY HALL. Historians Leonard and Dale Pitt describe Union Passenger Terminal as "the last of the great American railroad stations." Designed by a consortium of the city's architects headed by Donald B. Parkinson, the station comprises a group of one-story, stucco, tile-roofed buildings dominated by a 135-foot observation and clock tower. The structure is a highly artistic rendering of Spanish Colonial Revival architecture with a Moderne sensibility. The handsome interior has a 52-foot tall ceiling, marble floor, tall arched windows, and superb California tile ornamentation.

UNION STATION COURTYARD. Careful attention was given to space planning throughout the Union Station complex. Brick-patterned walks, light standards, and landscaping were carefully woven into a composition that integrated indoor and outdoor space through a Moderne interpretation of Mediterranean architectural elements.

UNION STATION RESTAURANT. The decorative details in this interior space—patterned ceiling, extensive use of tile, and decorative metal grill work—work in harmony with decorative use of architectural structure revealed in piers and arches. This unity of detail and structure is a fundamental design principle apparent throughout the station complex.

41

PASADENA FREEWAY TUNNEL. The Figueroa Tunnel through Elysian Park is on the Arroyo Seco Parkway, a six-mile throughway from downtown Los Angeles to Pasadena. Both freeway and parkway in its conception, the scale and detailing of its bridges and tunnels, as well as it location in a park system, suggest a Sunday drive rather than a daily commute. With its sunburst design, Figueroa Tunnel was one of several concrete entrances through Elysian Park that were styled in the Streamline Moderne.

HOLLYWOOD FREEWAY. The Hollywood Freeway, completed in 1948, ran from downtown Los Angeles through Hollywood to the San Fernando Valley, which was then experiencing exponential post World War II population growth. The road was engineered with four lanes in each direction, functional and banked curves, paved shoulders, and extended access lanes. A true freeway, it had few landscaping or parkway features.

DOWNTOWN FREEWAYS. This view of the downtown freeways looks east toward City Hall. At the center is the "stack," or four-level interchange connecting the harbor, Pasadena, and Hollywood Freeways.

Five

AVIATION
THE LURE OF FLIGHT

In the period between 1908 and 1915 an intense public interest was aroused in everything aeronautical, and it became a matter of civic pride to hold an airplane exhibition. These events were held so that spectators could see flying machines in action and build confidence in the future of aviation. Exhibitions of stunt flying brought thousands to sites which often were little more than dirt fields. The rival Curtiss and Wright teams generated publicity and attendance with extravagant prize money. Postcards were usually on sale and nearly every aviator had one standard postcard for sale.

The period between the World Wars was characterized by great aviation races and the building of airfields, as aviation travel became commonplace in American life. Public airports took over private facilities and airlines competed for passenger commerce.

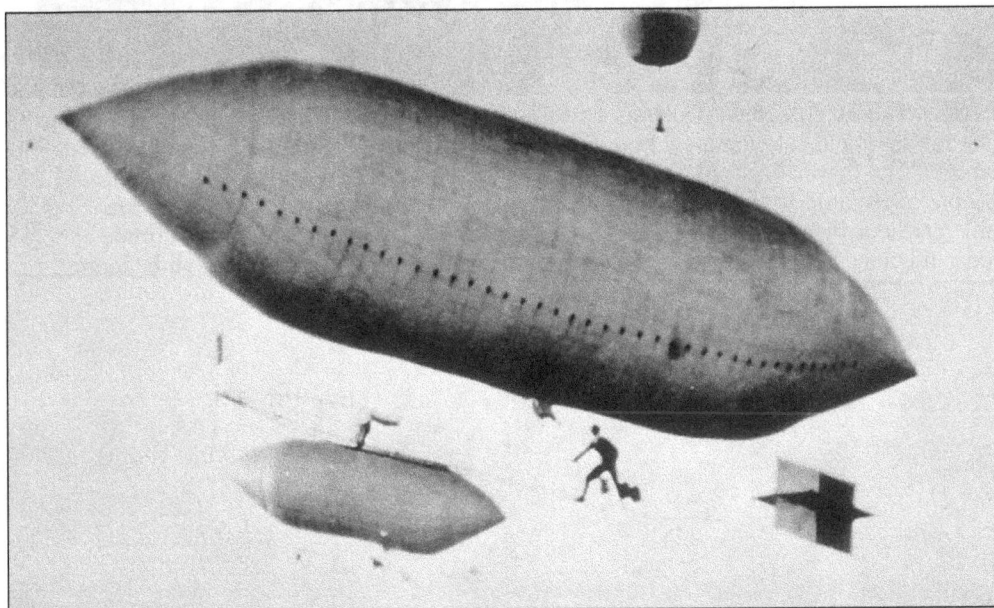

THE GREAT DIRIGIBLE RACE. This picture documents the great dirigible race between Roy Knobenshue and Lincoln Beachey, early barnstormers who were a popular feature at local dirigible exhibitions. Beachey later became the most famous American stunt flyer, stating that he had entertained 17 million people in 126 cities. A native of San Francisco, he crashed at the Panama Pacific International Exposition in his native city in 1915 when the wings of his plane sheared off during an ascent from a nose dive.

INTERNATIONAL AIR MEET DOMINGUEZ FIELD. Dominguez Field was the site of the country's first international aviation meet from January 10-20 in 1910. Historians Leonard and Dale Pitt report, "The mayor declared a city holiday and the spectacle was attended by some 175,000 people." Spectators in the 2,000-seat grandstand saw Glenn Curtiss make a record-breaking 50-mile-per-hour flight. Pilot Louis Paulhan earned $50,000 for climbing to an altitude of 4,165 feet, and pioneer woman skydiver Georgia Broadwick parachuted from a hot air balloon.

CHAPLIN, DEMILLE, AND ROGERS AIRFIELD, 1921. In 1919 director Cecil B. DeMille, excited by the possibilities of flight, teamed with Charlie Chaplin and the Rogers Aviation Company to form a company to fly mail by air. Although Mercury Aviation's visionary scheme did not succeed, the airfield, amid the oil derricks and bean fields of the Hancock Rancho La Brea land, was the site of air shows, stunt flights, and movie shots.

CURTIS WRIGHT FLYING SERVICE. Grand Central Air Terminal opened in Glendale in 1929 and was the premier airport in Southern California until the advent of jets in 1955. The first transcontinental flight from Southern California to New York originated at Grand Central with Charles A. Lindbergh as pilot. Curtiss Flying Service operated the airport and a technical school for repair and maintenance as well as modification of planes and engines. Maintenance Building, Hanger No. 1, a handsome example of California Mission Revival style, no longer exists, although the former airport terminal building and tower remain.

UNION AIR TERMINAL BURBANK, C. 1940. In 1928 Boeing Air Transport Company developed Boeing Air Field in Burbank in a sandy loam vineyard with giant oak and eucalyptus trees. A dry riverbed ran through the center of the property. In 1930 the airport was dedicated as United Airport and opened on Memorial Day with a three-day air show featuring exhibition flights of Boeing P-12 Pursuit planes and Keystone bombers. In 1934 the facility was renamed Union Air Terminal, Burbank.

MINES AIRFIELD. In 1928 the city of Los Angeles leased 640 acres of agricultural land near present day Westchester to build an oiled landing strip and 2 hangars to house 20 planes each. The small airfield expanded throughout the 1930s and became the Los Angeles International Airport after World War II. This official photo documents the competitor's positions at the National Air Races on September 15, 1928.

Four

UPTOWN, DOWNTOWN, AND OUT BROADWAY

Early significant buildings in the downtown area such as the Garnier Building and the Hellman Bank exemplified the spirit of the downtown business establishment whose preferences, together with the skill of their architect-designers, created monumental and elegant revival style buildings with Beaux-Arts, Romanesque, and Classical elements. The new buildings used pattern book elements with an original flair to showcase designers' talents and their clients' businesses. Cultural institutions such as churches, auditoriums, and parks worked together in a mixed pattern of uses to civilize the environment and ameliorate the haste, labor strife, noise, and traffic that accompanied everyday life.

By the mid 1920s Los Angeles' new array of downtown buildings gave the city an air of prosperity and civic dignity, but it was the structures of the 1930s like the Richfield Building that attracted nationwide attention. Art Deco and Art Deco Moderne suited a city still building its downtown. A casual observer walking down Broadway or traveling by street railway would have been most impressed by the lively mix of styles that had been created in the short span of three decades.

DESTRUCTION OF THE TIMES BUILDING, FIRST AND BROADWAY. The bombing of the *Los Angeles Times* Building, shown on this 1910 postcard, attracted nationwide attention. In the Romanesque Revival style characteristic of many early downtown buildings, the structure was destroyed during a protracted labor struggle initiated by *Times* founder Harrison Gray Otis. The blast killed 20 men and injured 17 others.

51

HELLMAN BANK. This flower-decorated postcard, *c.* 1910 with the Hellman Bank at center, demonstrates the elements of the good life to be found in Los Angeles: sound financial institutions, an impressive downtown skyline, and "one of Los Angeles' pretty parks." Judging by the city's growth, the offer of a prosperous business community, an impressive architectural environment, and a landscape of flowers, grass, and trees in the sunshine was difficult to resist.

LOS ANGELES TRUST AND SAVINGS BANK BUILDING. The marble banking suite of Los Angeles Trust and Savings Bank occupied the entire first floor of the 11-story Beaux Arts building at the northeast corner of 6th and Spring. Designed by architects Parkinson and Bergstrom, the structure has frontage of 60 feet on Spring and 165 feet on 6th Street.

GARNIER BLOCK, LOS ANGELES AND ARCADIA STREETS. The Garnier Block, now part of El Pueblo de Los Angeles State Historic Park, was built in 1890 in proximity to the original city Plaza, in what was then a predominately Chinese neighborhood. An example of early brick construction with sandstone trim and carved entrance, the building has been restored to its original appearance, although the south wing was destroyed in 1950 when the Santa Ana Freeway was built.

FOURTH AND MAIN STREETS. The Roman Revival bank shown in this postcard presents its elaborate temple-front entrances on both Fourth and Main. The intersection was the heart of Los Angeles' financial district in the first decade of the 20th century. The view shows the sharp incline of Fourth Street as it climbs toward Bunker Hill.

TEMPLE SQUARE. The International Bank Building and Post Office.

PHILHARMONIC AUDITORIUM AND OFFICE BUILDING. This post card view shows the 1906 Auditorium Building which housed offices, Temple Baptist Church, and the Philharmonic Orchestra, long supported by philanthropist William Andrews Clark, Jr. Grateful music lovers in Los Angeles commissioned a bronze statue of Beethoven, dedicated it to Clark and placed it in Pershing Square Park facing the Philharmonic Building. The monument still stands looking north across Fifth Street though the building was demolished in 1985.

FIFTH AND SPRING LOOKING WEST This panoramic view taken in 1913 looking down on Fifth Street illustrates the local custom of landmarking buildings on the sides and rear with business names and services.

56

GENERAL VIEW OF SIXTH STREET, METHODIST CHURCH ON LEFT. Like many Eastern cities, Los Angeles built an array of downtown churches. First Methodist Church is shown in this 1910 postcard opposite Pershing Square Park, comfortable among its business block neighbors. The structure no longer exists.

PERSHING SQUARE. Pershing Square, bounded by Fifth, Sixth, Hill, and Olive Streets, is shown in this postcard c. 1920, looking southwest across the Square. Design, hardscape, and landscaping of the park have changed over time. Postmodern architect Ricardo Legoretta added a new fountain and 125-foot campanile in a 1994 renovation.

PERSHING SQUARE FOUNTAIN. A view of the center of Pershing Square Park c. 1930. Water flows over the sculptured figures of four cherubs into a large pool. In this era, the Park featured brick paving, palm shaded walks, large banana plants, and wood benches.

THE EASTERN COLUMBIA BUILDING

This major Zigzag Moderne building features a stepped back design and terra cotta sheathing in gold and blue-green. A neon-lighted clock face appears on each of the four sides of the tower. The building originally housed two retail stores separated by an L-shaped arcade with entrances on South Broadway and West Eighth Street. Pierced grills stippled in gold in a sunburst pattern are the structure's most prominent decorative feature.

OVIATT BUILDING The Zigzag Moderne elements of the Oviatt attracted much attention. At its dedication the structure was described as "Ultra Modern," and the owners boasted that the shop front and marquee, as well as other interior work, was produced in France, shipped to Los Angeles and installed by French engineers and architects. Lalique glass was a feature of the external storefront.

PACIFIC MUTUAL BUILDING. A postcard view of the original Parkinson & Bergstrom-designed Pacific Mutual Building on Sixth Street. A six-story, white-glazed, terra cotta structure with a Corinthian Greek temple front, it was dwarfed by later neighboring buildings and then remodeled by the successor Parkinson firm in Moderne style in 1938.

SUNKIST BUILDING. "Sunkist" was the trade name for the California Fruit Growers Exchange. Architectural historians Harriette Von Breton and David Gebhard describe the massive Sunkist Building with its relief sculpture and entrance murals as "American Perpendicular" style. With setbacks for light and air at the third, fourth, twelfth, and thirteenth floors, it was designed to be entered from an automobile. The massive structure was the headquarters for a California agricultural giant that eventually controlled 70 percent of the state's citrus fruit crop. The Exchange, like the Automobile Club of Southern California, was enormously influential in the creation of the California tourist image of the pleasure-filled life and bounty of California. The structure was demolished when the company moved its corporate headquarters.

BROCK AND FEAGANS, BROADWAY. Brock & Feagans advertised themselves as the "Finest Jewelry Store in the West." Ornate and highly detailed with a rhythmic 4-bay facade, the building with its canopied entrance suggests a jewel box.

FINE ARTS BUILDING. The 12-story Romanesque-Revival style Fine Arts Building was constructed as office and studio space for artisans. Its ornate exterior with twisted columns, bracketing, and elongated arched windows is completed by a magnificent two-story lobby with sculptural figures representing the arts. The decorated wall panels are the work of celebrated Los Angeles tile maker Ernest Batchelder.

THE RICHFIELD BUILDING. The shimmering, black, terra cotta walls with gold-strip accents of the Art Deco Moderne Richfield building symbolized the "black gold" of oil. Considered the finest example of Los Angeles' Art Deco Moderne, it was designed in 1928 by Morgan, Walls, and Clements. The company demolished the structure in 1972 to make way for two larger buildings on the site.

RICHFIELD BUILDING DETAIL.
This close-up view of the bronze elevator doors in the Richfield Building demonstrates the level of quality in materials and design that characterized the structure.

THE SOUTHERN CALIFORNIA EDISON BUILDING (ONE BUNKER HILL) UNDER CONSTRUCTION. The elaborate steel frame of the 12-story Edison Building shows its futuristic massing and one-story pavilion entrance addressing the northwest corner of Grand and West Fifth Streets. Built in 1930-1931, the Art Deco building integrates art and architecture with lobby murals and entrance relief panels depicting Hydoelectric Energy, Light, and Power.

Spring Street, "Wall Street" of the West. The five-story Moderne gray granite building in the foreground was built in 1929 as the Pacific Coast Stock Exchange.

PACIFIC COAST STOCK EXCHANGE. The Stock Exchange Building is entered through two 12-foot high bronze doors. The fluted pilasters separate bas-reliefs above the entrance. A bull and a bear flank the central panel *Finance*; the left panel is *Research*; and the right, *Production*. Italian-born sculptor S. Cartaino Scarpitta, who worked extensively in the city on churches and monumental buildings, carved the composition.

BROADWAY BETWEEN FIRST AND SECOND STREETS. This view of Broadway, *c.* 1940, shows a solid and prosperous business street with a mixed low-rise-high-rise streetscape.

SECOND AND BROADWAY. Broadway between Second and Third Streets is captured here at a lull in the usually bustling traffic pattern. Overhead trolley and street railway lines show that the intersections was an important transfer point. Upper Broadway lacked major department stores or large office buildings so congestion increased as the traveler moved south.

FOURTH AND BROADWAY.

FIFTH AND BROADWAY. Its rush hour as street cars, pedestrians, and motorists vie for the right of way

BROADWAY WITH CHRISTMAS DECORATIONS. Broadway merchants traditionally suspended
Streets to enhance the holiday spirit and encourage shoppers to buy presents.

stars, wreaths and banners across the street and decorated street lanterns from Fifth to Eighth

W.P. STORY BUILDING. The white terra cotta facade of the 1910 Story Building by Morgan and Walls at Sixth and Broadway has elaborated columns and decorative cornices and brackets on the upper stories. In 1934 Morgan Walls and Clements remodeled the ground floor, covering up its Beaux Arts facade and creating an Art Deco metal gate in the entrance to the parking garage.

BROADWAY, STREET CAR PLATFORMS. To speed up the flow of traffic and keep pedestrians from injury, busy corners had raised cement platforms on which riders could stand to board and depart from the street railway cars.

BROADWAY AND TWELFTH STREET AFTER SNOWSTORM. Snow in Los Angeles in February was unusual enough to warrant the creation of this postcard, presumably to send back to the folks in colder climates to show that it wasn't always sunny and warm in Southern California.

THE GENERAL PETROLEUM BUILDING. General Petroleum, designed in 1949 by Wurdman and Becket, began the stylistic shift in downtown buildings to the International Style. Aluminum fin sunshades provided exterior decoration on the facades and operated as climate control. The architects accented building corners with a group of horizontal bezeled windows on each floor. The company logo, a flying horse, decorated the setback roof parapet.

Seven

CAR CULTURE

"Los Angeles," announced an early auto show room banner, "where the car is king." Los Angeles became motorized as soon as there were cars to be driven off the assembly line. In 1914 Henry Ford located his first California factory near the west bank of the Los Angeles River at Santa Fe and Seventh Streets. Workers sent Model T's down the line until 1930 when the plant moved to the Port of Los Angeles.

The oil that greased the wheels had long been an essential part of California life. Native Americans recovered it from tar sumps to waterproof their baskets and canoes; Californios of the pueblo distilled it for their lamps. After the Anglo-American settlement, furious drilling in oil wells promoted one of the many get-rich-quick Los Angeles fantasies: find oil in your own backyard—or front yard. Some did find the fabled black gold, while others sold it along with gas and tires in service stations which could often be found on all four corners of an intersection. Dealers sold automobiles on dusty lots and in fancy showrooms, purposely built in high architectural style to entrance buyers and enhance the mobile lifestyle. The Automobile Club of Southern California, originally a touring association for hardy travelers, had 30,000 members by 1920. "The language of design, architecture and urbanism in Los Angeles," wrote architectural critic Rayner Banham, "is the language of movement.

Center of LOCKWOOD AUTO COURT - 70 Cottages

LOCKWOOD AUTO COURT NEAR LINCOLN PARK. The auto court—an early day version of the motel—welcomed tourists and often provided a few weeks of accommodation for those just getting started and getting used to the traffic jams on downtown streets.

GENERAL VIEW OIL WELLS. The oil derricks pictured on this postcard were a familiar feature of the Los Angeles landscape in the first decades of the 20th century. Unsightly, noisy, and dirty, they were tolerated, if not loved, for their useful contribution to the culture of the car.

OIL WELLS AND PALM TREES—RESIDENTIAL AREA WEST OF DOWNTOWN. Though an intrusion on the land, oil wells lived happily among high-style homes with landscaped front yards. To have a comfortable home, a palm tree and oil well offered a vision of the California Dream.

77

RICHFIELD SERVICE STATION WITH FULL SERVICE ATTENDANTS. The Richfield Company under the hood of this motorist's fine 1948 Chevy Fleetline two-door sedan.

chose an imposing Classical Revival style to shelter the pumps and attendants that checked

SIGNAL OIL STATION TWENTY-NINTH AND VERMONT. This neat service station designed in authentic California Mediterranean Revival architectural style advertised itself discreetly with its center tower and miniature campanile.

PACKARD SHOWROOM, 1626 WILSHIRE BOULEVARD, 1928. The front of this elegant romantic Spanish Colonial Revival style building with its red tile roof and Spanish metal grillwork was designed with full facade glass windows so that cars displayed on its floor could be seen from the roadway. One of several ornate Packard showrooms in the city, it architecture was intended to persuade discriminating automobile purchasers that this was the place to buy a prestigious car to drive down the Boulevard.

AUTO CLUB OF SOUTHERN CALIFORNIA, 1923. Designed by Los Angeles architects Hunt & Burns in 1923, the Automobile Club of Southern California is an architectural landmark of the West Adams district. The most important institution in the development of car culture in Southern California, the club provided a multitude of services from erecting stop signs to legislative lobbying. California drivers still find indispensable "Triple A's" most popular program: roadside towing and repair for untimely breakdowns.

WILSHIRE AND VERMONT LOOKING EAST TOWARD BULLOCK'S WILSHIRE. Despite the operation of an enormous public transportation system of street cars and buses, the car soon became the most popular mode of travel. The results were predictable: congestion, traffic jams, accidents, and parking tickets. The unforeseen consequence of economic growth brought about by the car was the city's decentralization and the development of suburban housing.

Eight

DEPARTMENT STORES
LET'S GO SHOPPING

A wayward member of the flapper generation, reproved by her mother for failing to go to church, replied, "Oh, Mother, really. You go to Trinity Methodist; I'll go to Robinson's." As social historians have observed, department stores were the cathedrals of the 20th century, and Los Angeles was blessed with retail establishments that catered to every taste and purse. These early monuments to trade drew their customers downtown through the attraction of the variety of goods they offered and their appeal to the pleasure of the experience. One just got dressed up and went downtown; it was seen as an obligation, both to the self and the social group.

HAMBURGER'S DEPARTMENT STORE. With this postcard Hamburger's Department Store advertised its location at corner of Eighth and Broadway and showed off its handsome cast iron first story and mezzanine, below glazed terra cotta walls. Designed by Los Angeles' leading Beaux Arts architect, Alfred F. Rosenheim in 1907, the building was the first store in the city whose interior had been crafted for distinct departments.

J. W. Robinson Co., Seventh and Grand, showing Brockman Building, Los Angeles, Cal.

J.W. ROBINSON COMPANY. Merchandise was a little "higher" at Robinson's Department Store located at Seventh and Grand Street, west of the concentration of department stores on Broadway. These postcards document management's intention to keep an up-to-date image with high-style architecture. Originally a Moorish fantasy of pressed brick and terra cotta with ornamented corner towers, the structure was remodeled in 1936 into a smoothly polished composition by stripping away ornament to uncover the tower's structure and applying flat Moderne panels at the mezzanine story.

BULLOCK'S DEPARTMENT STORE. John G. Bullock opened his downtown store in 1906. Extending the length of the block on Seventh between Broadway and Hill Streets, Bullock's was a venerable Los Angeles retailer. A typical turn-of-the-century Beaux Arts structure, its architectural interest depends on the pattern of window openings and the strength of the corner tower. The extent of the building seems to assure the viewer that the supply of goods inside will surely include just what is needed.

BULLOCK'S WILSHIRE. In his new Wilshire Boulevard Store, John Bullock hired architects John and Donald Parkinson to design the quintessential Art Deco Zigzag Moderne design for shopping in the city of the future. Massing, materials, ornament, and the new building's copper-sheathed tower signaled a new approach in city retailing. No longer a part of a compact downtown streetscape, the new structures displayed their sophistication in lavish exterior and interior ornament.

BULLOCK'S WILSHIRE, EXTERIOR MOTOR COURT. Bullock's Wilshire was designed to be easily entered from the rear porte cochere where customers handed off their cars to a parking attendant. No expense was spared in the decoration of this motor entrance, which featured a ceiling mural entitled, "The Spirit of Transportation." The central figure is Mercury surrounded by a Graf Zeppelin, ocean liner, railroad train, and early passenger airplane.

Harris and Frank Clothing Store. Harris and Frank's distinctive vertical window treatment above the ground display windows was designed to bring natural light into mezzanine offices and fitting rooms on the second and third floors.

Nine

TRADEMARK
LOS ANGELES

Architectural critic Paul Gleye describes programmatic architecture as "the ultimate in swift visual impact." The trick was to shape buildings, or to model their decoration, according to what the owner wished to sell. In a place where there was much land, many small buildings, and a multitude of small business, it paid to utilize the building to insure that the establishment would be seen and remembered.

Los Angeles architects often had a more graceful and subtle program: Period Revival architecture. American society required acculturation: a quick settlement into communities. Revival architectural elements offered familiar symbols of a humanistic past that many shared despite their varied backgrounds and cultures. Revival styles were certainly not the exclusive province of Los Angeles builders and designers, but their mastery of the idiom grew out of the desire to utilize the past to express an original aesthetic for the growing city.

FEDERAL BANK OF LOS ANGELES. The 1910 Federal Bank of Los Angeles at Avenue 22 and North Broadway just across the North Broadway Bridge in Lincoln Heights, is a notable example of early Period Revival building. The designers used the corner lot to advantage, showcasing the elegant, Italian Renaissance-inspired center dome that commanded a view of the river.

LOS ANGELES EXAMINER BUILDING. Commissioned in 1915 by William Randolph Hearst and
iron, and plaster work; an impressive lobby with patterned-tiled floors and elaborate friezes. When
efficient qualities those pleasing traits reminiscent of an architecture that is identified with the

designed by Julia Morgan, The Examiner Building featured Mission arches, loggias, ornamental the building was complete, Hearst wrote, "I am glad to note the building combines with its beautiful and romantic history of Los Angeles and California."

VAN DE KAMPS BAKERY. Perhaps the best known and most loved of Los Angeles' trademark commercial structures were the Van de Kamps windmill bakeries with clerks costumed in "Dutch Girl" uniforms and hats.

HEINSBERGEN BUILDING. Los Angeles artist and decorator Tony Heinsbergen commissioned this building in 1927 for his workshop and offices. During his long career, Heinsbergen created murals for more than 700 theaters. His trademark compositions were elaborate colored stencils and painted decoration on ceilings of grand homes, hotels, and important downtown office buildings.

SAMSON TYRE AND RUBBER COMPANY. The Samson Tyre Factory, located on a heavily traveled arterial boulevard, put its best face forward. Architects Morgan, Walls, and Clement created a fabricating plant surrounded by magnificent walls that spared motorists an unlovely view of the manufacturing process. Samson Tyre was in the best tradition of programmatic architecture: uniting building and product forever in the public mind. A sympathetic adaptive reuse has preserved the property, and the 1,700 foot "Assyrian" walls now enclose a large shopping center.

GOODRICH BUILDING. This beautifully maintained composition of lawn and trees in an industrial setting demonstrates the commitment that early builders made to landscape. Land was not a scarce commodity and water was imported in abundance. Community spirit demanded that the streetscape and building grounds be cultivated.

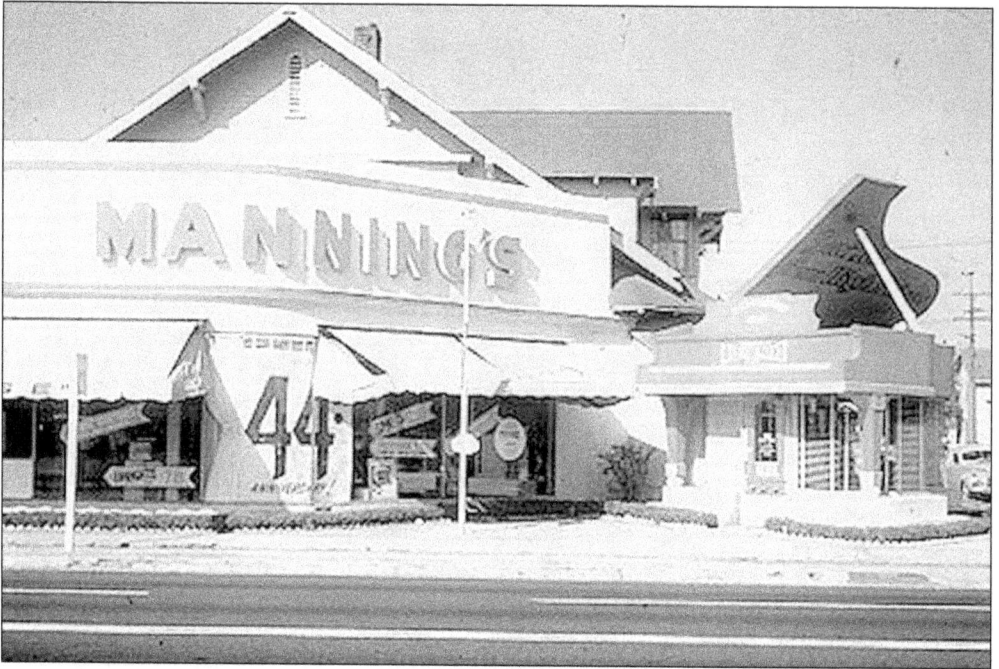

MANNING'S PIANO STORE. Manning's, at the corner of Pico and Oxford in Los Angeles, had no shyness in advertising their presence and product. A splendid example of programmatic architecture, The Big Red Piano Store looked as much piano as store.

MODE O'DAY BUILDING. Mode O'Day manufactured moderate-priced women's clothing, marketing its goods in its own retail outlets throughout the western United States, usually on the main streets of small towns. Mode O'Day's clothes were comfortably mid-Western, without the glamorous image of Southern California fashion.

Ten

EATERIES

The movie stars went to the Brown Derby on the cook's night off. The folks liked cozy neighborhood restaurants. The kids loved the drive-in, which symbolized the spirit of the city. "Googie," Los Angeles coffee shop architecture of the late 1940s and 1950s, made signage an integral element of the building. Architects slanted walls to accommodate broad areas of plate glass, and jazzed interiors with hot orange vinyl and cool chrome. Los Angeles' had become a low-rise, horizontal, auto-oriented city, and the new style expressed its energy.

BROWN DERBY RESTAURANT. The original Brown Derby on Wilshire Boulevard at Alexandria Street, Los Angeles' preeminent example of programmatic eateries, was famous throughout the world. Dependent on the patronage of the high-finance world of Hollywood deal making and the glamour of stars and their studios, the restaurant could not survive the change in the industry that accompanied the end of the studio system and the rise of independent film making.

Mona Lisa Café. This attractive postcard showed potential diners that a double pleasure awaited them when they visited Mona Lisa restaurant at Seventh and Coronado Streets: an Italian dinner in the spotless restaurant and an interesting tour of courtyard shops afterwards.

St. Bernard Café. St. Bernard Cafe advertised itself on this 1938 postcard as a "Tyrolese" restaurant. Another draw to patrons and their families were the stuffed dogs in the windows.

St. Germain Restaurant. St. Germain Restaurant made good adaptive reuse of this imposing Craftsman bungalow when its Third Street neighborhood began to develop into a commercial thoroughfare.

CARPENTERS DRIVE-IN. In the 1930s, drive-in architecture symbolized the spirit of the city:
Western Avenue combined the comfort and privacy of eating in the car with the fun of going
order area, canopy, and the neon-lit tower that functioned as a sign, diverting cruising and

motion, machines and modernism. Carpenter's Drive-In at Wilshire Boulevard and
out. Typical of late 1930s drive-ins, it had a simple three-element program: the central kitchen
and drivers to the scene.

CLIFTON'S CAFETERIA, SIXTH AND OLIVE STREETS. Each Clifton's Cafeteria had its own theme. The Pacific Seas branch on Sixth and Olive Street in downtown Los Angeles featured flowing waterfalls and indoor humidity for exotic tropical plants. Civic reformer Clifford Clinton arrived in Los Angeles during the Great Depression. With the motto, "pay what you can," he opened the first of his chain of seven cafeterias in July 1931, providing free meals to those who could pay nothing.

COFFEE DAN'S. A somewhat subdued and early version of Googie architecture, Coffee Dan's emphasized structure and signage. Essentially an A-Frame with large expanses of wall glass, the eatery relied on its shape and roof decoration to attract passing motorists.

100

Eleven

MARKETS

Despite population growth and speculation, land near the city remained in agricultural use well into the 20th century, making Los Angeles the leading county in the nation in farm production. Produce growers, poultry raisers, and orchardists also raised exotics and specialty crops. Whether trucked into wholesale markets or delivered directly to retailers, food in abundance was available to the city's residents throughout the year.

MARKET ON BROADWAY. While signage in this Broadway market is certainly independent of the building's architecture, the owner and customers alike must have enjoyed the tall windows that lighted the interior.

PIGEON RANCH. Almost anywhere one looked in Los Angeles County, some sort of agricultural enterprise was underway and squab was in demand for banquets and fancy dinners. This Southern Pacific Coast Line railroad postcard allowed passengers to show those at home early California agribusiness.

PRODUCE MARKET. The Central Avenue market was the main wholesale produce terminal for Los Angeles. Horses and wagons are still in use, but the postcard shows that trucks have begun to take over transport and distribution.

FARMER'S MARKET, THIRD AND LA BREA. A traveling gourmet's delight, the Farmer's Market at Third and La Brea Streets is one of the most popular and enduring Los Angeles institutions. During the Great Depression, Earl Gilmore allowed area farmers to sell their produce on a portion of Gilmore Oil Company Land. In time the Gilmore Company took over the project, building a drive-in market with open-air stalls and several fixed buildings in the American Colonial Revival style. Farmers Market's landmark windmill on a wooden tower was replaced by a less rustic clock tower with the market's name on a weathervane.

LOS FELIZ MARKET. Although architect H. Roy Kelley's designs usually incorporated references to historic architecture, they were functionally modern in massing and plan. In this 1933 market on Vermont Avenue, the simplified Moderne exterior provided the backdrop for the boldly stylized lettering, advertising with both aesthetic and commercial appeal.

CHAPMAN MARKET. An authentic 1929 Los Angeles drive-in market, Chapman Park Market was a collection of stores set in a closed quadrangle entered from the street. Inside, an open-air courtyard provided spaces for parking. Its decoration was the Churiguerresque detail characteristic of Spanish Colonial architecture.

Twelve

THEATERS
LETS GO TO THE MOVIES

Los Angeles may have been consumed by the cult of the car, but it was in the movie theater that the fantasy of gold paint, murals, and dazzling light sconces on the walls surpassed the fiction on the silver screen. In downtown Los Angeles' gilded auditoriums, stars forever shone. On Broadway, the Los Angeles Theater had its own building with architecture so wondrous that even those without a dime for the movie, got a nickel's worth of joy from the ornamentation of the building. As the town grew outward from downtown, more modest theaters arrived in the neighborhoods, but the tradition of the grand movie house did continue on Hollywood Boulevard.

THE PALACE THEATER ON BROADWAY. The Palace Theater, on Broadway between Sixth and Seventh Streets, was a 1911 design by architect G. Albert Lansburgh, for the Orpheum Vaudeville Circuit. The Palace enlivened the streetscape with its facade of polychrome terra cotta arches by sculptor Domingo Mora. Lansburgh was the principal architect of theaters on the West Coast from 1900–1930.

STATE THEATER. The State Theater on Broadway at Seventh Street was built in 1921 for the Loews Circuit. This structure's contribution to the elegance of the Broadway Theater district is the elaborate "silver platter" chased ornament above the ground story.

LOS ANGELES THEATER. The grandest example of theater decoration in downtown Los Angeles, the Los Angeles Theater, designed in 1931 by S. Charles Lee, is regarded as the master of movie palace expressionism. Classical grandeur and Baroque ornamentation were applied with the utmost exuberance.

LOS ANGELES THEATER INTERIOR. Architect Lee is said to have modeled the opulent interior of the Los Angeles after the Hall of Mirrors in Versailles. A crystal fountain was placed at the head of the grand staircase. The theater had a restaurant and a ballroom on the lower levels.

THE AVALON ENTERTAINMENT COMPLEX, CATALINA ISLAND. The nine-story, steel reinforced, Art Deco Avalon Casino, c. 1929, has a theater with a full working stage and a famous circular ballroom on the top floor. At one time, visitors taking the ferry from the mainland could dance in the casino by night and by day watch spring training by the Chicago Cubs baseball team, then owned by Catalina Island's developer William Wrigley Jr. The 110-seat theater has a renowned Wurlitzer organ still used for Sunday concerts.

INTERIOR OF THE AVALON THEATER. In the interior of the Avalon Theater, Art Deco light fixtures highlighted fantasy murals painted by artist John Gabriel Beckman. When his original painted murals in the outer foyer were damaged by sea air, Beckman crafted them in tile.

MAYAN THEATER. The Mayan Theater was designed in the heyday of Period Revival building in Los Angeles. Instead of following European and Near Eastern stylistic precedents, it derived its style from the American hemisphere, using the decorative arts of Southern Mexico and Central America for the theme. Architects Morgan, Walls, and Clement provided owners with a plain-front building. Artist Francisco Cornejo was hired to decorate the building.

WARNER BROTHERS BUILDING AND PANTAGES THEATER. The imposing Warner's Building dominated the northwest corner of South Hill and West Seventh Streets with twin facades extending from its corner tower. The landmark round dome atop the tower guided theatergoers to the Pantages Theater below.

THE ACADEMY THEATER. Also an S. Charles Lee theater design, the Academy is a landmark in Streamline Moderne design. The rolling stucco cylinders of the base, glass block, ticket booth, and Art Deco lettering are meticulously crafted details of a composition directing focus to the tower. Its spiral fins were originally lit by blue neon tubes.

Thirteen

LET'S DRIVE OUT
ON WILSHIRE

Although Los Angeles had flourished by reliance on the Pacific Electric and Los Angeles Electric Railways, by 1920 the automobile was becoming the most influential factor in the official and private planning decisions of its residents. Linear development was the operative choice as development moved westward and Wilshire became the commercial boulevard. Development accelerated when Wilshire was extended through McArthur Park. In the decade of the 1920s, many of the downtown department stores opened branches or moved to the five-mile section between the Park and Fairfax Avenue.

WILSHIRE BOULEVARD AND WESTERN AVENUE. This view of Wilshire Boulevard, looking west up Wilshire, shows the Pelissier Building and Wiltern Theater on the left. The Wiltern, a Los Angeles Art Deco Zigzag Moderne masterpiece with turquoise terra cotta sheathing, was designed by Albert Lansburgh with interior by Anthony B. Heinsbergen. When built, it housed the largest theater organ in the United States.

LAFAYETTE PARK AND VIEW OF WILSHIRE BOULEVARD. Lafayette Park, a small, landscaped hollow of winding walks and lawns, features a Shakespeare Fountain and the decorative brick and stone Felipe deNeve Branch Library. This view looking southeast down Wilshire Boulevard shows the Town House and the tower of Bullock's Wilshire in the distance. Wilshire Boulevard only changes direction between Los Angeles' downtown and Beverly Hills once, at Hoover Street, after passing commonwealth Avenue at the Town House's southeast corner.

THE MIRACLE MILE. The Miracle Mile was a prestigious shopping center on Wilshire Boulevard west of downtown. Developer A.W. Ross conceived this portion of Wilshire Boulevard as an Art Deco linear retail center of prestige department stores offering free parking and saving the buying public a trip downtown.

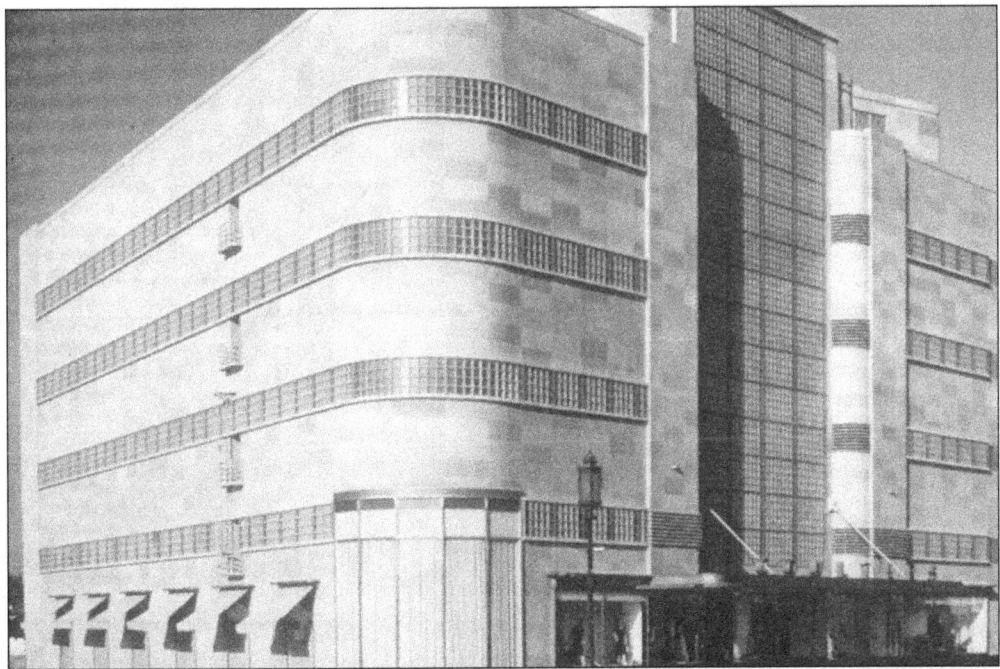

COULTER'S DRY GOODS COMPANY. Developer Ross persuaded Coulter's, which had been downtown on Seventh and Olive, to close its downtown operation completely and move to the Miracle Mile. The company built an impressive new Streamline Moderne building in its new location. The structure was demolished in 1980.

WILSON BUILDING. The Wilson building was sited at the corner of Wilshire and La Brea and designed with large areas of plate glass wrapping around the first and second stories. Architectural historian Paul Gleye, quoting the journal *Architect and Engineer* in 1930, states, [the Wilson building offers] "an opportunity for the tenants to appeal to the great number of people passing the building in machines."

116

Fourteen

CONSTRUCTING CULTURE
PORTRAITS OF DIVERSITY

Always the good and bad times contrasted bitterly in the city's human record, but the artists, activists, and ordinary people of Los Angeles worked side-by side to construct the culture of the city. Los Angeles has always had many races and creeds, laboring to find a foothold in the city's economy and win a place in the community. In the course of that struggle, those forced to create a separate community made their lives a record of service that enriched the city beyond measure. "Shape clay into a vessel," says the Chinese sage, "it is the space within that makes it useful." In the building spaces of their city, Angelenos created the metropolis, then in the next moment thrilled at the adventure of climbing skyward to look down upon it.

THE MONTENEGRO FAMILY. The language, culture, and customs of the Hispanic citizens of Los Angeles have been a continuous legacy to the city. Pride in family and tradition are evident in this portrait of the Montenegro family sons and daughters, who posed for a group portrait with their mother Carmen in 1917.

LOS ANGELES CITY ENGINEER'S SURVEY TEAM. The City Engineers Survey Team stands in front of Old City Hall with the tools of their trade. The diversity of population in Los Angeles at the turn of the 20th century is evident in the faces of the workmen whose labors laid out the city's street grid and boundaries.

ENGINE NO. 30, LOS ANGELES FIRE DEPARTMENT. Old Fire Station 30, now the home of the African American Firefighter Museum, was established in 1913 to serve the Central Avenue community. The museum opened in 1997, the centennial of the induction of George W. Bright, Los Angeles' first African American firefighter, into the Los Angeles Fire Department.

NELLIE KAY CARLISLE. A pioneering African American resident of Los Angeles, Nellie Kay Carlisle was valedictorian of the Polytechnic High School Class of 1915. The wife of a decorated World War I infantryman, she was commissioned a captain in the California Women's Communication Corps in World War II, commanding the Newton Street Company, which manned the air raid warning post in the Los Angeles Memorial Coliseum.

BETTY AND BETSY. The Rhee twins, Betty and Betsy, Los Angeles natives, enjoy some moments of fun before their freshman year at Belmont High School in 1942. The Rhee family were pioneers in the small Korean community in Los Angeles before World War II. The Korean presence in Los Angeles would grow to over a quarter of million people by 1990.

TEMPLE, TERMINAL ISLAND. Prior to relocation in internment camps at the beginning of World War II, a thriving colony of Japanese Americans lived and worked on Terminal Island in the Port of Los Angeles. This Shinto temple, *c.* 1915, was built by the community.

CANNERY WORKERS, TERMINAL ISLAND. Jean Watasuki Houston, in her memoir *Farewell to Manzanar*, recalls Terminal Island's cannery workers reported to the packing plants whenever the blast of the whistles alerted them to the arrival of the boats. "One for Stokely's; two for Van Camp's," brought workers down to the processing sheds day or night.

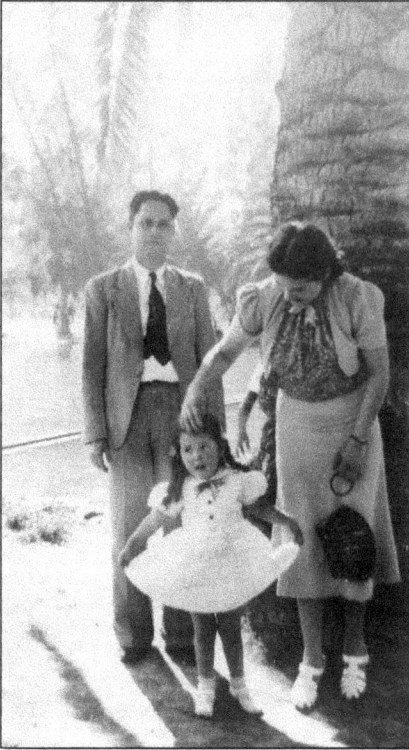

THE GOMEZ FAMILY AT LINCOLN PARK, 1937. Lillie Gomez poses in the shade of a palm tree with her parents, Catalina and Esteban, at Lincoln Park in East Los Angeles.

LILLIE GOMEZ ON THE DAY OF HER QUINCEANERA. One of the most important traditions in the Hispanic community is the Quincenera, a combination 15th birthday party and debut celebration. Lillie Gomez celebrates the occasion in 1950, posing in the auditorium of the International Institute. Founded in 1914, the Institute was dedicated to promoting understanding among varied ethnic and racial groups.

RICHARD KEYS BIGGS. Biggs was a celebrated Los Angeles organist who toured the world. Referred to as "The High Priest of the Temple of Tone," Biggs was a serious musician whose artistry brought the organ into the musical consciousness of the concert public. After a town hall recital, *American Organist Magazine* wrote, "We rank him with the elite at the top, and bid him enter his challenge for first place. . . He has supreme poise."

AIRPLANE PASSENGER. This happy flyer who had just returned from a spin on one of the many hour-long pleasure flights that Angelenos could take to experience the thrills of flight, marked the occasion with two snapshots mailed to a friend. On the back of this picture, the message reads, "Here I am just as we landed; the pilot helping me off the plane. Just a small step."

PLEASURE FLIGHT. On the back of this photo the passenger wrote, "I took this picture just before landing. We waved to the other passengers in their plane. I will run over to see you soon so be prepared. Bye."

HARRIETTE CARR VON BRETON. An artist, art collector, political activist, and architectural historian, Harriette Carr Von Breton worked at Disney Studios and then moved into the worlds of politics and social service. A leader of the Los Angeles Chapter of the League of Women Voters and member of the Democratic State Central Committee, she also served on the boards of the Los Angles Child Guidance Clinic and Booth Memorial Home. She collected East Indian art and lectured on architectural history at the University of California Santa Barbara. She served on the Board of the Society of Architectural Historians and with David Gebhard co-authored the seminal volume on Los Angeles' Moderne architectural styles, *Los Angeles in the Thirties*.